AF425917

FISHY FUNNIES

VOLUME ONE

FISHY FUNNIES

BY N BLAKE SEALS
ARTWORK BY MEAGHAN "MAYFLOWER" SEALS

EDITED BY VINCENT FERRANTE
DESIGN AND EDITORIAL PRODUCTION BY BLAKE

FISHY FUNNIES VOLUME ONE PUBLISHED BY MONARCH COMICS.
ISBN 979-8-9894602-3-6

MONARCHCOMICS.COM

THAT'S ONION. AND THAT'S COW.
THEY'RE TWO GOLDFISH THAT LIVE ON A SHELF IN A HIGH SCHOOL
BIOLOGY CLASS. THE KIDS IN THE CLASS NAMED THEM.

MY DAUGHTER, MEAGHAN, WHO USES THE MONIKER 'MAYFLOWER'
ON SOCIAL MEDIA, DREW THEM ON HER IPAD AND CREATED A
LITTLE VIRTUAL BOWL FOR THEM.

I COLLECT RIDICULOUS JOKES FOR ONION TO TELL HIS PAL COW.
SOMETIMES MEAGHAN'S SISTER MADISON BRINGS ONE TO THE
TABLE - OR TO THE BOWL, I GUESS YOU COULD SAY.

AND THAT'S IT. THEN WE PUT THEM IN A BOOK. THIS BOOK.

IT'S OK...YOU CAN LAUGH WHILE YOU ROLL YOUR EYES.

-BLAKE

APPLIED
GEOMETRY

HEY, COW, WHY DID THE MATH BOOK LOOK SO SAD?
UM, WHY?
'CAUSE OF ALL OF ITS PROBLEMS!

HEY, COW...
WHY CAN'T A
NOSE BE 12 INCHES
LONG?
REALLY, ONION?
WHY NOT?
BECAUSE THEN IT
WOULD BE A FOOT!

YO, COW, WHAT'S BROWN AND STICKY?
AH, GEEZ, ONION, WHAT?
A STICK!
OH, C'MON!

WHY CAN'T YOU HEAR A PSYCHIATRIST USING THE BATHROOM?
UH...WHY?
BECAUSE THE P IS SILENT!

HEY, COW.
WHAT DO YOU CALL AN
ELEPHANT THAT DOESN'T
MATTER?
I DON'T CARE.
AN IRRELEPHANT!
CAN YOU JUST
GO AWAY?

I ONLY KNOW 25 LETTERS OF THE ALPHABET.
HUH? WHY?
I DON'T KNOW Y.

HEY, COW, WHERE DOES SCOTT LIVE?
I DON'T KNOW, ONION. WHERE?
SCOTLAND.
I'M GETTING ANOTHER FISHBOWL.

HOW DOES THE MOON CUT HIS HAIR?
ECLIPSE IT.
HEY! THAT'S MY LINE!

WHAT DID ONE WALL SAY TO THE OTHER?
WHAT?
I'LL MEET YOU AT THE CORNER.

HEY, COW. WHERE DO FRUITS GO ON VACATION?
WHERE?
PEAR-IS!
UGH.

WHAT DID BABY CORN SAY TO MAMA CORN?
I DON'T KNOW.
WHERE'S POP CORN?

NNESS

HEY COW, WHAT COUNTRY'S CAPITAL IS GROWING THE FASTEST?
I DON'T KNOW.
IRELAND. EVERY DAY IT'S DUBLIN.

DID YOU HEAR ABOUT THE GUY WHO INVENTED THE KNOCK-KNOCK JOKE?
UM, NO.
HE WON THE NO BELL PRIZE.

YO COW. WHAT'S THE BEST SMELLING BUG?
AH JEEZ, WHAT?
A DEODOR-ANT.

Barilla
FARFALLE
SERVING SUGGESTION

WHAT DO YOU CALL A FAKE NOODLE?
COME ON, ONION, WHAT?
AN IMPASTA.
UGH.

UCKER'S
SEEDLESS
rawberry
Jam

HEY COW, WHAT HAPPENS WHEN A STRAWBERRY GETS RUN OVER CROSSING THE STREET?
OH, NO. WHAT?
TRAFFIC JAM.

HEY, WHAT DO YOU CALL A FISH WEARING A BOWTIE?
WHAT?
SOFISHTICATED.
YOU LOOK RIDICULOUS.

WHERE DO YOU LEARN TO MAKE A BANANA SPLIT?
HUH? I DON'T KNOW. WHERE?
SUNDAE SCHOOL!

HEY, COW, WHY DO SEAGULLS FLY OVER THE OCEAN?
UM...WHY?
BECAUSE IF THEY FLEW OVER THE BAY, WE'D CALL THEM BAGELS.

HOW DO YOU GET A SQUIRREL TO LIKE YOU?
I HAVE NO IDEA, ONION. HOW?
ACT LIKE A NUT!
EASY FOR YOU TO SAY.

YO! YO! COW!
WHAT, ONION?
WHAT DOES A LEMON SAY WHEN IT ANSWERS THE PHONE?
WHAT?
YELLOW!
UGH.

WHAT DO YOU CALL CHEESE THAT ISN'T YOURS?
WHAT?
NACHO CHEESE.
ONION, YOU'RE AN IDIOT.

COW?
YEAH?
WHY DID THE SCARECROW WIN AN AWARD?
HE DID? WHY?
YEP! BECAUSE HE WAS OUTSTANDING IN HIS FIELD!

WHAT DO YOU CALL IT WHEN A SNOWMAN THROWS A TANTRUM?
WHAT?

A MELTDOWN.

WHERE DOES BATMAN GO TO THE BATHROOM?
HUH?

THE BATROOM.

HEY, COW.
WHAT DO YOU CALL
A PONY WITH A SORE
THROAT?
I DON'T KNOW.
A LITTLE HORSE.

COW, HOW DO CELEBRITIES STAY COOL?
I DON'T KNOW, ONION, HOW?
THEY HAVE A LOT OF FANS.

SO,,,WHY DON'T SHARKS EAT CLOWNS?
WHY?
BECAUSE THEY TASTE FUNNY.

HEY, COW...
WHY DON'T WE EVER
SEE ELEPHANTS HIDING
IN TREES?
WHY?

BECAUSE
THEY'RE REALLY
GOOD AT IT.

WHAT DO YOU CALL A BELT MADE OF WATCHES?
WHAT?
A WAIST OF TIME.
ONION, YOU'RE A WASTE OF MY TIME.

YO - COW - WHY IS PETER PAN ALWAYS FLYING?
GOOD GRIEF, ONION. WHY?
'CAUSE HE'S FROM NEVERLAND.

I WOULD NEVER BUY ANYTHING WITH VELCRO.
WHY NOT?
IT'S A TOTAL RIP-OFF.

WHAT DID THE OCEAN SAY TO THE BEACH?
WHAT?
NOTHING. IT JUST WAVED.

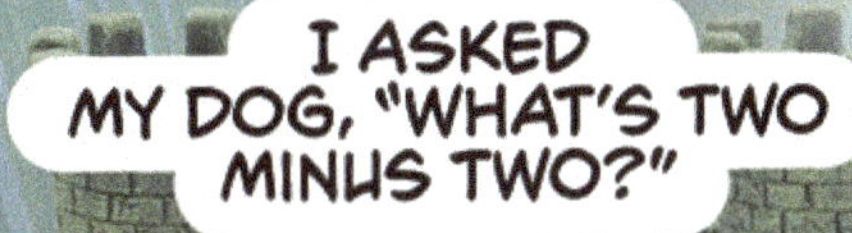

I ASKED MY DOG, "WHAT'S TWO MINUS TWO?"
WHAT DID HE SAY?
HE SAID NOTHING.
YOU DON'T EVEN HAVE A DOG.

HEY, COW. WHAT DOES A SPRINTER EAT BEFORE A RACE?
UH...WHAT?
NOTHING, THEY FAST!

YO, COW. WHERE DO BOATS GO WHEN THEY'RE SICK?
WHERE?
TO THE BOAT DOC.

WHAT KIND OF CAR DOES AN EGG DRIVE?
WHAT?
A YOLKSWAGON.

SO, COW...
HOW DOES A PENGUIN
BUILD ITS HOUSE?
HUH? HOW?
IGLOOS IT
TOGETHER.

WHAT DID THE SNAIL WHO WAS RIDING ON THE TURTLE'S BACK SAY?
UM, WHAT?
WHEEEEE!

WHAT DID THE LEFT EYE SAY TO THE RIGHT EYE?
UM, WHAT?
BETWEEN YOU AND ME, SOMETHING SMELLS.

SO, COW...
HOW MUCH MONEY
DOES A PIRATE PAY
FOR CORN?
DON'T KNOW,
ONION, HOW
MUCH?
A BUCCANEER.

COW, WHERE DO YOUNG TREES GO TO LEARN?
I GIVE UP. WHERE?
ELEMENTREE SCHOOL.

WHAT DID THE PIRATE SAY WHEN HE TURNED 80?
UM...WHAT?
AYE MATEY!

HEY, COW! DID YOU HEAR THE RUMOR ABOUT THE BUTTER?
NO! WHAT IS IT?
WELL, I'M NOT GOING TO SPREAD IT

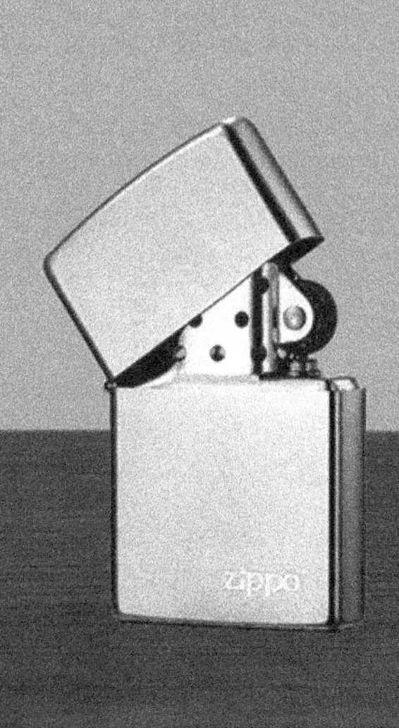

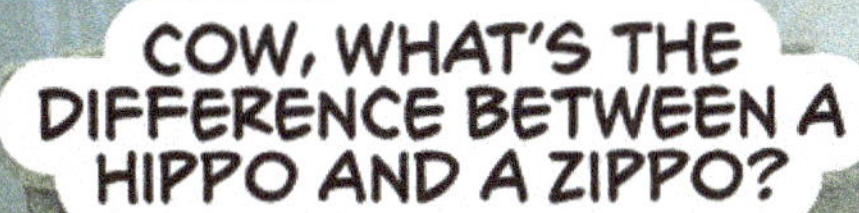

COW, WHAT'S THE DIFFERENCE BETWEEN A HIPPO AND A ZIPPO?
I DON'T KNOW, WHAT?
ONE'S PRETTY HEAVY AND THE OTHER IS A LITTLE LIGHTER.

HEY, COW - HAVE YOU HEARD THE ONE ABOUT THE ROOF?
NO, WHAT IS IT?
NEVER MIND. IT'S OVER YOUR HEAD.
ONION, YOU'RE A JERK.

WHAT DO YOU CALL TWO MONKEYS THAT SHARE AN AMAZON ACCOUNT?
WHAT?
PRIME MATES.

HOW CAN YOU TELL IF A TREE IS A DOGWOOD?
UM, HOW?
BY ITS BARK.

FLAVOR
OTTLE
nch's
E 1904
ssic
LLOW
STARD
CIAL FLAVORS
14 OZ (396 g)

WHAT DO YOU CALL A HOT DOG ON WHEELS?
AH, GEEZ, ONION, WHAT?
FAST FOOD!

WHAT'S THE BEST WAY TO WATCH A FLY FISHING TOURNAMENT?
HOW?
LIVE STREAM.

ALSO AVAILABLE
EVIL MONKEY MEMES
EXPANDED VOLUME ONE
& VOLUME TWO

MONARCHCOMICS.COM

amazon   BARNES &NOBLE

EVIL MONKEY
MEMES
EXPANDED VOL. 1
IF AT FIRST YOU DON'T SUCCEED
SKYDIVING IS NOT FOR YOU
N BLAKE SEALS

EVIL MONKEY
MEMES
VOL. 2
I COULD TELL YOU A JOKE ABOUT PIZZA...
...BUT IT'S A LITTLE CHEESY.
N BLAKE SEALS

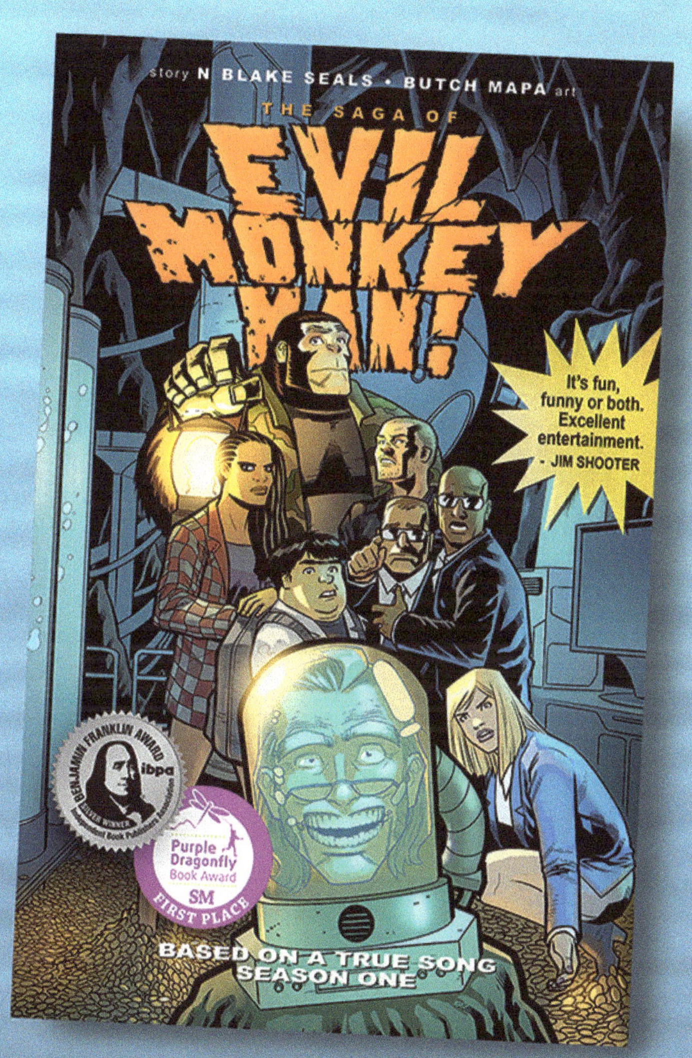

story N BLAKE SEALS • BUTCH MAPA art
THE SAGA OF
EVIL MONKEY MAN!
It's fun, funny or both. Excellent entertainment.
- JIM SHOOTER
BENJAMIN FRANKLIN AWARD
ibpa
SILVER WINNER
Purple Dragonfly Book Award
SM FIRST PLACE
BASED ON A TRUE SONG
SEASON ONE

EVIL
MONKEY
MAN!
TM
CHAPTER ONE
by N BLAKE SEALS & BUTCH MAPA

www.ingramcontent.com/pod-product-compliance
Lightning Source LLC
Chambersburg PA
CBHW041914130726
48007CB00015B/182